GREEN BAY PACKERS

ALL-TIME GREATS

PACKERS

BY TED COLEMAN

Book design by Jake Slavik
Cover design by Jake Slavik

Photographs ©: Rick Osentoski/AP Images, cover (top), 1 (top); Tony Tomsic/AP Images, cover (bottom), 1 (bottom), 11, 12; AP Images, 4; John Lindsay/AP Images, 6; Vernon Biever/NFL Photos/AP Images, 8; David Stluka/AP Images, 14, 16, 18; Morry Gash/AP Images, 21

Press Box Books, an imprint of Press Room Editions.

ISBN
978-1-63494-356-7 (library bound)
978-1-63494-373-4 (paperback)
978-1-63494-406-9 (epub)
978-1-63494-390-1 (hosted ebook)

Library of Congress Control Number: 2020952630

Distributed by North Star Editions, Inc.
2297 Waters Drive
Mendota Heights, MN 55120
www.northstareditions.com

Printed in the United States of America
082021

ABOUT THE AUTHOR

Ted Coleman is a sportswriter who lives in Louisville, Kentucky, with his trusty Affenpinscher, Chloe.

TABLE OF CONTENTS

CHAPTER 1
THE FIRST CHAMPIONS

The Green Bay Packers are one of the oldest teams in the National Football League (NFL). In fact, the team was created before the NFL even existed. The Packers were an early dynasty. They won three NFL titles in a row from 1929 to 1931. **John McNally** was the star of those teams. McNally went by his nickname, "Johnny Blood." He was a colorful character and an outstanding running back. He could also catch, pass, and play defense.

Arnie Herber was the team's first great quarterback. The Green Bay native led the NFL in passing yards and touchdowns three times.

HUTSON
14

Football experts consider Herber one of the
NFL's first modern passers. He influenced the
many others that came after him.

Herber tossed many of his passes to wide receiver **Don Hutson**. In Hutson's day, the NFL was built around running. But with his skills as a receiver, Hutson helped begin an era of passing. He ran precise routes like modern receivers. When he retired, he held most major receiving records.

Tony Canadeo began his career doing it all for the Packers. He played offense, defense, and sometimes even punted. After serving in World War II (1939–45), Canadeo played running back. In 1949, he became the third player ever to rush for 1,000 yards in a season.

CHAPTER 2

THE LOMBARDI ERA

The Packers were dominant in their early years. But in the 1950s, they were one of the worst teams in the NFL. In 1959, Green Bay hired a little-known head coach named **Vince Lombardi**. Right away, the Packers posted their first winning record in more than a decade. Lombardi went on to lead the greatest era in Packers history.

Running back **Paul Hornung** was named Most Valuable Player (MVP) in 1961. He helped the Packers win their first NFL championship in 17 years.

Fullback **Jim Taylor** was a physical, aggressive runner who wore down opponents. He earned MVP honors in 1962 as the Packers won another NFL title. Taylor scored Green Bay's lone touchdown in the title game on a freezing-cold day in New York.

Blocking for those great backs was offensive tackle **Forrest Gregg**. Gregg was tough and durable. At one point, he played 188 games in a row. He helped open up holes and protect the quarterback.

CAREER RUSHING TOUCHDOWNS
PACKERS TEAM RECORD

Jim Taylor: 81

STARR

15

That quarterback was the legendary **Bart
Starr.** He was the league's MVP in 1966. That
year, the Packers qualified for the very first

PACKERS HALL OF FAME

The Packers of the 1960s had some of the most talented rosters in NFL history. Lombardi coached 13 Hall of Famers. Eight of them played on all five championship teams. They were Herb Adderley, Willie Davis, Forrest Gregg, Henry Jordan, Jerry Kramer, Ray Nitschke, Bart Starr, and Willie Wood.

Super Bowl. Starr was MVP of that game, and the Packers easily beat the Kansas City Chiefs. Starr won the Super Bowl MVP again the next season, and Green Bay repeated as champs. In his 16 years with the Packers, Starr lost only one playoff game.

The Packers could play defense, too. Linebacker **Ray Nitschke** was one of the hardest hitters in the NFL. He was also a great athlete. He intercepted 25 passes during his career. These Hall of Famers, with a Hall of Fame coach leading them, won five championships in seven years.

FAVRE

4

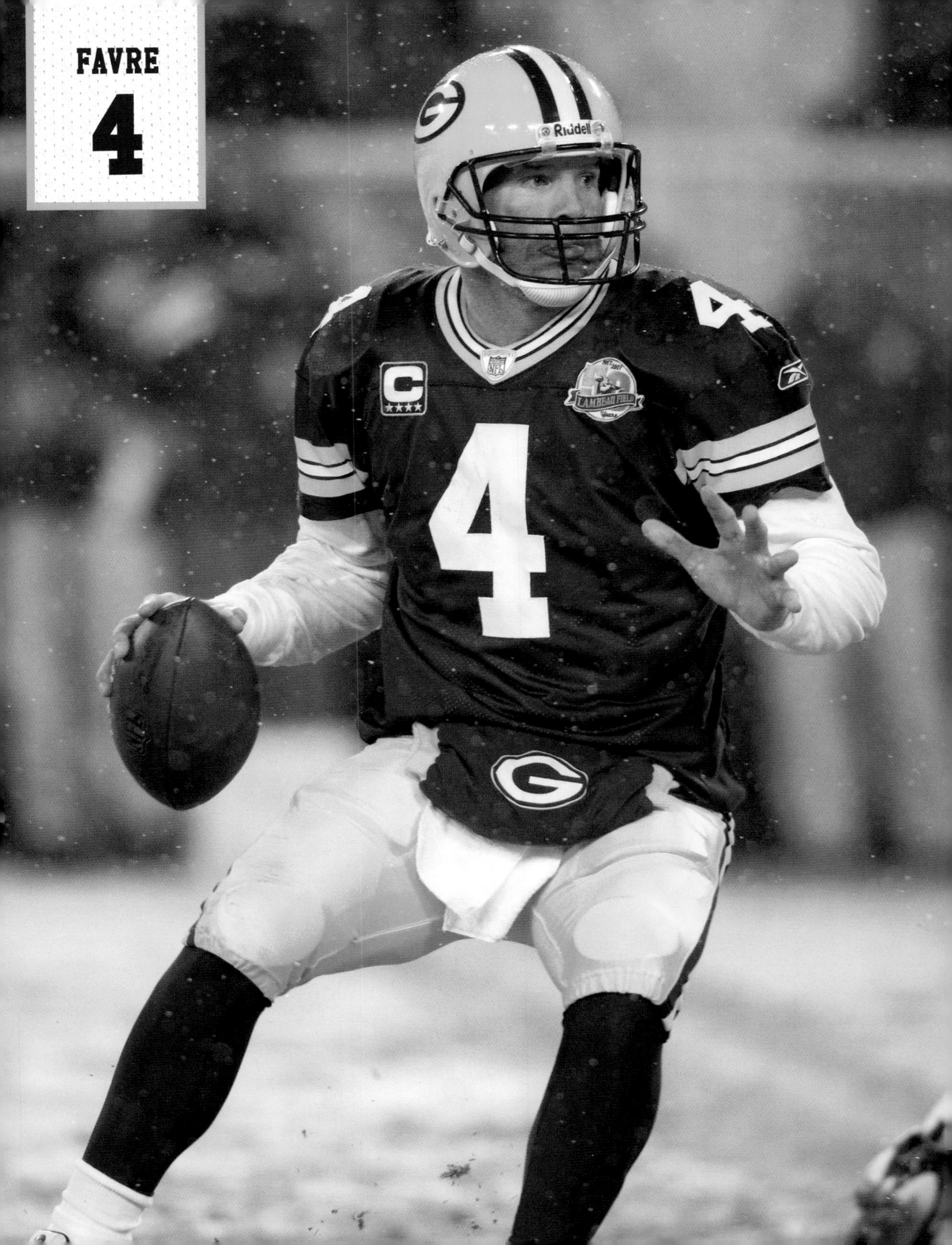

CHAPTER 3

THE FAVRE ERA

After Lombardi left, the Packers struggled for two decades. But everything changed in 1992. That was the year Green Bay traded for **Brett Favre**. The young quarterback was a risk-taker with a cannon for an arm. Favre went on to win three MVP awards. And in the 1996 season, he led the Packers to their first Super Bowl title in 29 years.

STAT SPOTLIGHT

CONSECUTIVE STARTS
NFL RECORD
Brett Favre: 297

DRIVER
80

Favre threw to great receivers such as **Sterling Sharpe** and **Donald Driver**. In 1992 and 1994, Sharpe led the NFL in receiving touchdowns. Driver arrived in 1999. He went on to become Green Bay's all-time leader in receiving yards.

MIKE HOLMGREN

After many years as an assistant, **Mike Holmgren** finally became a head coach in 1992. That was the same year Brett Favre joined the team. Together, Holmgren and Favre reached two Super Bowls, winning one.

Running back **Ahman Green** racked up the yards on the ground. From 2000 to 2004, no NFL player had more rushing yards. In all, Green ran for 8,322 yards as a Packer. That was the most in team history.

Green Bay also had a tough defense led by **Reggie White**. The powerful defensive end tormented opposing quarterbacks from 1993 to 1998. Meanwhile, safety **LeRoy Butler** was a force in the secondary. Butler invented the famous Lambeau Leap in 1993. He returned a fumble for a touchdown and then jumped into the stands to celebrate. The Lambeau Leap soon became a tradition after touchdowns.

RODGERS
12

CHAPTER 4
THE RODGERS ERA

After Favre left in 2007, the Packers didn't have to wait long for their next legendary quarterback. **Aaron Rodgers** was already on the team. He spent three years as a backup, but he became the starter in 2008. Rodgers quickly turned into a superstar. He was the Super Bowl MVP in the 2010 season. And he was named the NFL MVP in 2011, 2014, and 2020.

The 2010 team was anchored by defense. Its leader was **Charles Woodson**. The veteran cornerback came to Green Bay in 2006. In 2009, he was named Defensive Player of the Year. The next season, he broke his collarbone during the Super Bowl. At halftime, he gave an emotional speech. It helped inspire his teammates to victory.

Linebacker **Clay Matthews** was Green Bay's other defensive leader. Matthews flew across the field, playing

MIKE McCARTHY

Mike McCarthy was Brett Favre's quarterback coach in 1999. By the time McCarthy returned to the team in 2006, he was the head coach. This time, he had another great quarterback in Aaron Rodgers. Rodgers and McCarthy won one Super Bowl together. McCarthy won 125 games during his 13 years as Packers head coach.

both inside and outside linebacker. In the Super Bowl, he forced a fumble that helped the Packers keep their lead. Matthews went on to become the team's all-time sack leader.

Wide receiver **Davante Adams** joined the Packers in 2014. He quickly became Rodgers's

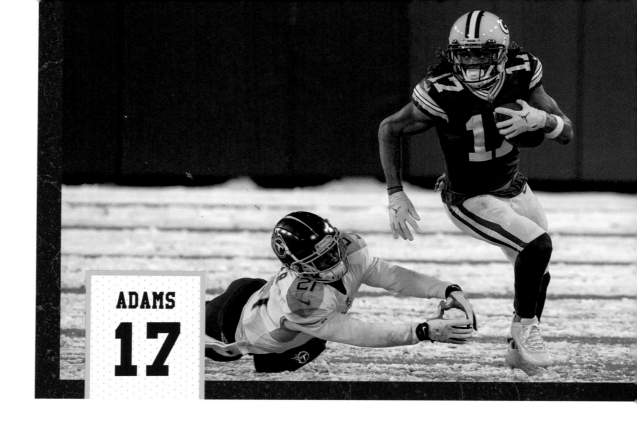

ADAMS
17

favorite target. In 2020, Adams tied a Packers record with 18 touchdown catches. From Starr to Rodgers, and from Hutson to Adams, Packers history is filled with legendary players.

CAREER SACKS
PACKERS TEAM RECORD
Clay Matthews: 83.5

TIMELINE

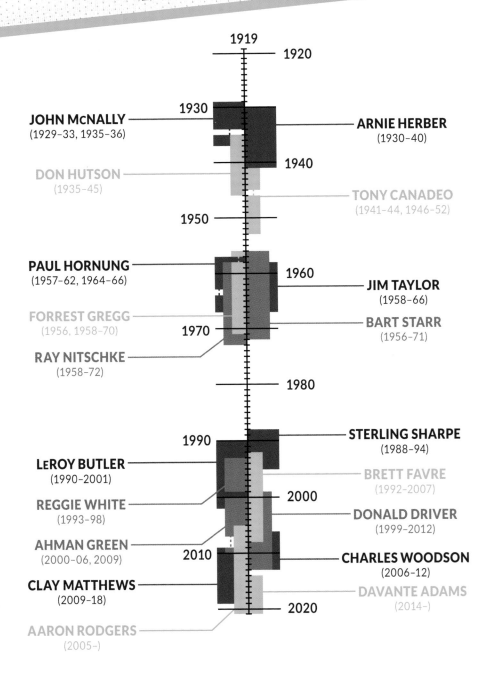

1919

1920

1930

JOHN McNALLY
(1929–33, 1935–36)

ARNIE HERBER
(1930–40)

DON HUTSON
(1935–45)

1940

TONY CANADEO
(1941–44, 1946–52)

1950

PAUL HORNUNG
(1957–62, 1964–66)

1960

JIM TAYLOR
(1958–66)

FORREST GREGG
(1956, 1958–70)

BART STARR
(1956–71)

1970

RAY NITSCHKE
(1958–72)

1980

1990

STERLING SHARPE
(1988–94)

LeROY BUTLER
(1990–2001)

BRETT FAVRE
(1992–2007)

REGGIE WHITE
(1993–98)

2000

DONALD DRIVER
(1999–2012)

AHMAN GREEN
(2000–06, 2009)

2010

CHARLES WOODSON
(2006–12)

CLAY MATTHEWS
(2009–18)

DAVANTE ADAMS
(2014–)

2020

AARON RODGERS
(2005–)

GREEN BAY PACKERS

Founded: 1919
NFL championships: 11 (1929, 1930, 1931, 1936, 1939, 1944, 1961, 1962, 1965, 1966, 1967)
Super Bowl titles: 4 (1966, 1967, 1996, 2010)*
Key coaches:

Curly Lambeau (1919–49), 209-104-21,
6 NFL championships
Vince Lombardi (1959–67), 89-29-4,
5 NFL championships, 2 Super Bowl titles
Mike Holmgren (1992–98), 75-37-0,
1 Super Bowl title
Mike McCarthy (2006–18), 125-77-2,
1 Super Bowl title

MORE INFORMATION

To learn more about the Green Bay Packers, go to
pressboxbooks.com/AllAccess.

These links are routinely monitored and updated to provide the most current information available.

*1966 through 2020

GLOSSARY

cornerback
A defensive player who covers wide receivers near the sidelines.

dynasty
A team that has an extended period of success, usually winning multiple championships in the process.

era
A period of time in history.

linebacker
A player who lines up behind the defensive linemen and in front of the defensive backs.

rushing
Running with the ball to gain yards.

sack
A tackle of the quarterback behind the line of scrimmage.

secondary
The defensive players who typically cover wide receivers.

veteran
A player who has spent several years in a league.

INDEX